Father and Son Relationship:
looking Towards the future

By MUSTAFA EL-AMIN

Published by:
El-Amin Productions
P.O. Box 32148
Newark, NJ 07102

Father and Son Relationship:

Looking Towards the Future

Table of Contents

Acknowledgement
Foreword

                                                              Page No.
Chapter 1
    Belief in a Supreme Being 1

Chapter 2
    A Son's Responsibility to His Father 4

Chapter 3
    Abraham and Ismail: An Excellent Example
    of Father and Son Relationship 7
    Ismail and His Father's Vision 8
    The Sacrifice 10
    Stand Upon Principles 11
    Abraham and Ismail Separated 11
    Father and Son Build the Kabah 12

Chapter 4
    Jacob and His Sons 15
    Jacob's Sons Response 18

Chapter 5
    Luqman's Advice to His Son 22

Chapter 6
    Knowledge and Education 24
        Formal Education 26
        Computers 29
        College 29
        Advice to the College Student 31

Chapter 7
    Open Communication 33
        At the Dinner Table 34
        Walk, Talk and Work 34
        Fear vs. Respect 35
        Do I Really Know My Son? 36
        Do I Really Know My Father? 36
        Human Excellence 38

Chapter 8
    The Link to the Father 40
    What Will You Leave Your Son? 40
    Conclusion 41

ACKNOWLEDGEMENTS

I would like to express my thanks and appreciation to all those who have had a positive impact on my life. My deepest gratitude goes to my father, although we did have a cordial relationship, he did provide me with a spirit of entrepreneurship and determination through his commitment to working for himself.

I would also like to thank my two life long friends, Umar Bey Ali and Ansari Nadir for their many years of friendship and brotherhood, as well as their advice and encouragement in preparing this book. And Zeotha Hameed, a dear friend and close companion in Islamic propagation. May Allah bless and reward him abundantly.

The works and efforts of the Father and Son, Men and Boys Association of Newark, New Jersey are greatly appreciated. A special thanks from the core of my heart goes out to Imam W. Deen Mohammed for his tireless work on behalf of humanity. I can never thank you enough for the benefits that I've received from your leadership. May Allah's fountain of abundance forever flow upon you.

Last but not least, I'd like to thank my wife, Wafiyyah and our children for their encouragement and patience. I'd like to give a little extra thanks to my eleven month old daughter Madinah.

FOREWORD

Father and son relationships are very special and unique. When such relationships are nourished so that they develop naturally and healthy, the result is as two eyes with one vision; "looking towards the future".

Father and son relationships are a precious gift from God. When a father and son is united by the keystone of love, respect and understanding they are like two mighty pillars upholding the family structure and society.

When I think of father and son relationships, the prophets David and his son, Solomon, come to mind. I've been taught that under David's leadership, the material for building a beautiful temple was gathered and that his son Solomon actually had the temple built. Some say that there were two pillars at the entrance of the temple, symbolizing past and future. Others believe that they allude to the material and the spiritual. I am inclined to believe that they represented father and son.

There has been a great strain and burden placed upon family life in general and father and son relationships in particular. More specifically, the African American family. After centuries of slavery, oppression, terrorism, and mis-education, the true role of father and son relationship has been lost for the majority of African American families.

Although there are still too many problems with father, son relationships, there seems to be a greater awareness of the problems and a commitment by concerned individuals and groups to seriously address the problems. It is my hope that this book will help such noble efforts.

The information and suggestions that are expressed in this book will help all of us look a little closer at our relationship with our sons and our fathers and see how we can improve that relationship. When we look at our children, we are actually looking at the future.

1
Belief in a Supreme Being

"Whatever is in the heavens and whatever is in the earth declares the glory of Allah: to Him belongs the Kingdom, and to Him belongs the Praise: and He has power over all things".

(Holy Quran 64:1)

Belief and Faith in the Creator of all things is the basis for developing healthy family relations. The human being can get profound guidance from such belief and faith because it helps create the proper attitude for handling family relations.

As a parent, it helps us to realize that we are not the Creator of our children, but only limited caretakers. And although we may want to walk with our children through every step of life in hopes of preventing them from walking into some of the pitfalls of this world, the reality is that we cannot, therefore belief and trust in Allah gives us the sense of security that is needed. What we must do is give our children as much sound advice as possible.

God created us and our children, and each of us have a purpose and a destiny. As individuals we must try to find our purpose and reach our destiny. As parents we must do all that we can to help our children find their purpose and reach their destiny. We must try to make the road as smooth as possible. We must first realize that our children, their soul, their mind, their total being has a purpose and a destiny. Their purpose and destiny will not be identical to the parents. It may complement ours, but it's not identical. Allah says in the Holy Quran: *"To each is a goal to which he turns . . ."* (2:148). Allah also says: *"Verily, (the ends) you strive for are diverse."* (92:4).

Our ultimate goal is to Allah and our aim is to please Him. Sometimes we travel different roads to get to the same destination.

Our children are a great blessing and responsibility that Allah has entrusted us with. They are a creation of Allah and are created in excellence and must be nourished and guided by adults until they reach adulthood.

If we do all that we can to instill in our children, from the earliest stages of their life, the belief and faith in a Divine Creator, Who governs and rules the entire Creation, then we will have a strong foundation upon which we can maintain good family relations. As fathers, we must let our sons know that Allah created them and us, and that we are responsible for many things as men and that they have some responsibilities themselves as our children. Allah is going to hold us all responsible for what we are charged with. We are not self-created nor are we responsible for our form. Allah says, *"He created the heavens and the earth with truth and He formed you. Then made excellent your forms, and to Him is the ultimate resort."* (64:3).

2

The Son's Responsibility to the Father

As a son, it is important that you realize that your father is or was someone's son and that he had to grow and develop just like you are growing and developing. His circumstances were different but the process of human development is the same.

You were not on this earth before your father, therefore, there are some things that he has seen and experienced before you were born. Maybe what he has seen and experienced can help you.

Young man, it would be wise of you to try and learn as much as you can about your father and his life. It will help you, if not now, certainly in the future.

There is a reason why our fathers think the way they do and act the way they do. We may not like the way they do things. But at least try to understand it. Seek the understanding, pray for it. When the right time presents itself, talk to him about it. But always show respect. It is not always easy, most times, it is probably extremely difficult. But sometimes, it is not as hard as we might think. Allah tells us in the Quran, "Show kindness to your parents" (6:151)

In many cases, the children are living in a completely different world than their parents. The world is changing fast and it has been for years. But our worlds do not have to be completely separate. Respect and understanding will help us come together so that we can all benefit.

Life has been very difficult for African American people in general, and the African American male, in particular. Many of our people do not even know why they act the way they do. Their circumstances in this world have destroyed them. Your responsibility as a teenager or young adult is to try as hard as you can to make progress, to be positive. Do not pick up a crutch and just blame the White man or the system. Do not be blind to the evils in America, but strive hard to advance yourself in spite of the evils.

You may never know or understand why your father did or did not do something, that is why it is so important for us to believe and have faith in God. Because God can guide us out of any difficult situation. Also trust in your own abilities. God has made you an honorable and dignified being. He has equipped you to deal with the challenges of life. Use the intelligence that

God has given you. Be willing to listen and learn; that will help you grow.

Imam W. Deen Mohammed, speaking at a Business Conference in Newark, New Jersey on May 24, 1997, gave some advice that could lead one to unlimited success. He said "Trust yourself more, believe in yourself more that you can obey God and get the best use of your human resources. And don't let this world rush you. Stay comfortably with God, Allah and have faith and work hard with your tools and keep your faith . . . no matter what happens see it in God's Plan, see it in God's Scheme."

3

Abraham and Ismail: An Excellent Example of Father, Son Relationship

"And when his Lord tried Abraham with certain commands, which he fulfilled: He said: 'I will make you an Imam to the people.' He (Abraham) said 'and from my offspring'? He answered: 'But my covenant does not include the unjust'". (2:124)

The above verse from the Quran gives us a good picture of Abraham's character. He was a man who fulfilled his obligations. He was not a selfish person. He was not short-sighted. He did not reject leadership, responsibility. Abraham's concern about his future, his offspring is made very clear. God promised to raise Abraham's level of responsibility and He immediately asked about his offspring.

We can learn a profound lesson from this. As fathers, we

should be intelligent and look to the future. We should not only be concerned about the present. Allah tells us that we will find in Abraham an excellent pattern of conduct and those with him. (60:4).

In the book <u>Islam's Climate for Business Success</u> by W. Deen Mohammed, he writes, "God wants us to plan our future; He doesn't want us to have a situation where everything is by chance. We don't live by chance, we plan for our tomorrows. We are to plan for our children's tomorrows . . . Don't see your children as other than yourself. Your children are from you. Know that your "life" is in those children . . . Do not live, only for today. Our Prophet said 'Live Today as though you are going to live always'. I should plan to have what I will need for tomorrow and for the years down the road . . . Invision what you want for your children twenty years from today and have that as a plan. Plan to save money for your children's education" (pages 119, 120, 121).

Ismail and His Father's Vision

Most fathers hope that at least one of their sons will accept and carry their vision and their work forward. Most men would like for their sons to agree to help them in their work in some way. I don't necessarily mean their occupations. I am referring to their principles, their ideas, perhaps their family name, their philosophy, or religion, etc.

Intelligent people have dreams, hopes and a vision for a better future and they hope that their dreams and hopes will be realized one day. They know, however, that it can only be truly realized if someone else accepts to help carry it forward after them. The Quran gives us an interesting reference to how Abraham presented his vision to his son Ismail.

> *"Then when (the son) reached (the age) to work with him, He said: O my son! I have seen in a dream that I should sacrifice you; consider then what you see. He (the son) said: O my father, do what you are commanded; if Allah please, you will find me of the patient ones." (37:102)*

First, we see that Abraham's son had reached a certain point in his development before Abraham even discussed his dream with him. This suggests to us fathers that we should watch our children's development so that we can have some idea as to when we should demand and expect certain things of them. Sometimes you can say something to a person at one time and they don't grasp it, but if you say it, maybe a year later, they will grasp it. Abraham also showed respect for his son's ability to think and to see. He said, "consider then what you see". Do you see something else; is their another side to this?

We should encourage our children to share their views and visions on matters. Let them know that this is what you want them to do. Because our decisions as parents will affect the children as well as the entire family.

Ismail encouraged his father to do what he was commanded. In other words, carry out your vision, which you believe is from God and I will be patient with it, if Allah pleases. The key is patience. Fathers and sons must be patient with each other. Especially when the son gets older and he starts to feel a greater sense of self and independence. The father must be aware of the fact that he himself at some point in his life behaved in some way like his son or sons are behaving.

The Sacrifice

Abraham did not kill his son. His willingness to obey God and accept God as the authority in his life and over everything in creation, was enough.

Ismail accepted to be sacrificed on the strength of his love and trust in his father and his faith in God. *"So when the two of them submitted and he laid him prostrate on his forehead . . . We called out to him 'O Abraham! You have already fulfilled the vision; thus indeed do we reward the doers of good. Surely this was a clear trial" (37:103-106).*

Abraham and Ismail are used here to teach us a lesson. That we are not to kill our children. We are not to sacrifice their body, mind, spirit, soul, etc., even if they are willing to allow us to do it. We should love Allah so much until we are willing to do anything to please Him. And we should not let anything stop us. We should not think that we have to kill our sons for the pleasure of Allah. The Quran states *"It is not their meat nor their blood that reaches God. It is your regardfulness that reaches Him" (22:37).*

Stand Upon Principles

As men, fathers, we must establish rules of conduct and behavior. We must be consistent not haphazard. Establish regular patterns and follow them. This helps children sometimes better than you verbally telling them what to do. Make it clear that you have principles upon which you stand. If we live by those principles ourself then perhaps our children will do the same. Be firm and compassionate; firm but understanding and sensitive. Our sons need that.

Abraham and Ismail Separated

It is reported that Abraham left his wife, Hagar and their

son Ismail in the desert. Being the responsible person that he was, he left them provisions (food, water, etc.), which he thought would be enough until he returned.   However, according to the story, it was not enough, and Hagar, the mother went searching for water for their son Ismail. She ran back and forth seven times between the two hills of Safa and Marwa. She made a complete search. It is reported that the well of Zem Zem sprung up under Ismail's heel as he rubbed it back and forth on the ground and they both drank from it, thus saving their lives.

There are several lessons that we can get from this story. First, that there are some circumstances that can develop in our lives that may result is us being separated from our sons. Second, if that does happen, make sure that you leave some provisions. Some child-support. Give as much as you can. Make sure that your conscience is clear and your heart is at peace knowing that you gave as much as you could to help sustain your child's life. It may be that very child who doesn't live with you that may actually help you in building a better world.

Abraham and Ismail Build the Kabah

"And remember Abraham and Ismail raised the foundations of the house . . . " (2:127).

The Kabah, which is the focal point for all Muslims, the House, which we are obligated to visit at least once in our life, (if we can afford to) was built by a father and a son. It is called a house (Baitun); which suggest family life. It is also called a Masjid; the Sacred House of Worship. The word Kabah actually means joints, connections, inter-locking. The builders of the Kabah were two individuals that were connected and joined together based on blood ties. (Father and son). A family is a number of individuals joined together or connected and interlocked through blood ties.

The son who was separated from his father and almost lost his life in the desert with his mother, the son who was almost killed by his father turned out to be the one to help the father in his greatest work.

We should try very hard to include our sons in some of our work. Abraham included his son in the building of the Kabah. As sons, we should also try to help make the family and the world better. We should see ourselves as builders, building upon the foundation of our parents and fore-parents, materially and spiritually. If they were not able to leave anything physical upon which to build, then build upon their spirit, their hopes and aspirations, their goodness. We should make sure that we leave something material and spiritual upon which our offspring can build.

The Kabah was actually first built by Adam, but over a period of time, it was destroyed. That is why it is said that Abraham and Ismail "raised the foundation of the House". Abraham, Ismail and all human beings are the children of Adam. Two of his children, two prophets rebuilt the House that Adam originally built. *"We have honoured the sons of Adam" (17:70).*

One of the words for son/children in the Quran is directly associated with the word builder. They come from the same root (BNY).

4
Jacob and His Sons

"And Abraham enjoined upon his sons and so did Jacob; 'Oh my sons! Allah has chosen the Faith for you; then die not except as Muslims".
(2:132)

Jacob was one of Allah's prophets who was blessed with tremendous insight and faith. He was greatly concerned about his sons and the future generations. Upon his death he expressed his deepest concern to his sons. In the Quran it says *"Were you witnesses when death appeared before Jacob? When he said to his sons: 'What will you worship after me'? They said: 'We will worship your God and the God of your fathers, Abraham, Ismail and Isaac, one God and to Him do we submit"* (2:133).

Jacob like Abraham was a man of great faith and love of God. He was committed to worshiping the One God. He wanted to know that his sons were going to carry on his legacy.

When you are truly committed to an idea, a belief or philosophy, you shouldn't want it to die with you. Your hope should be that someone else will pick it up and carry it on.

Those of us who are Muslims, particularly African Americans, our concern should be the same as Jacob's and the other prophets and faithful believers of the past. Our struggle over the many years in America to gain respect and a broad acceptance of Al-Islam is a very serious thing. Our efforts to establish an Islamic community in America while at the same time trying to ease the fears of the American people, of Muslims, is very serious business. We should want to know that our children will carry that struggle on.

Muslims and other God-fearing people know that only God could have brought us through the vicious system of slavery that was established here in America. Only God could have turned our hearts to Al-Islam.

After being sold and kidnaped from Africa, placed in chains and stacked in the bottom of ships, like sardines, and taken across the Atlantic Ocean to America (called the Middle Passage), and made into slaves, sold on the auction block like animals, brutalized, tortured, humiliated and murdered; after all of that, to still embrace Islam, only Allah could have turned our hearts to Islam. Only God could have made us Muslims. The Quran states: *"Those who Allah desires to guide he opens their breast to Al-Islam"* (6:125).

For a people to be cut off from their homeland and their heritage, brainwashed, denied education and made to hate themselves and see themselves as inferior to all other human beings; made to worship a false image of God and forbidden to practice any of their native customs, tricked into hating their past, after all that; for many of us to become Muslims; for our hearts and souls to turn to Islam, is a blessing and miracle from God. We should cherish it, defend it and do all that we can to make sure that our children inherit it. We were cut off from our Islamic life and the oppressors did all that they could to keep us from re-connecting with our Islamic life. They did not want us to be Muslims. So who has made us Muslims? Allah! Who has allowed us to re-connect with our history? Allah, the Most High God!

As fathers, our most important concern should be, will our sons worship the One God. All other concerns are secondary to that, because if our children sincerely worship the One True God, Allah, everything else will fall into place; because God is the Provider, Sustainer and Protector. He is the one who opens all the doors of opportunity. As Muslims, we should be greatly concerned about whether or not our children are going to continue to be Muslims worshiping Allah, the Creator of all things.

Jacob's Sons' Responses

Jacob's sons gave their father the assurance that he was looking for. Not just to please Jacob, but because that is how they actually felt and believed. They believed like their father believed. In their youth, some of them did things that angered their father and might have made one wonder if they were ever going to get on the right track.

Jacob's sons did not only answer in the affirmative, they made it absolutely clear that they intended to worship the One True God. The same as their father Jacob, and his fathers, Abraham, Ismail and Isaac.

In analyzing the brief conversation between Jacob and his sons, we find an important characteristic of human nature. That is, the urge and desire to know. We don't know what will happen after we die. We don't know what the future holds for us and our offsprings. In the quiet of our hearts and minds, we want to know. Jacob wanted to know. How can I be sure that I've done my job as a father and a believer in the One God. As a parent, he yearned to know if his children would be all right after he was gone. It may have been a burden on him. When his sons told him that they were going to worship the One true God, it brought peace to his heart and soul. It eased his mind, because now he knew for sure that his sons would be all right and that his legacy would be preserved. Allah had mercy on Jacob and gave him a great reward.

We don't know what the future holds for any of us; but as parents we would like to have some kind of assurance that our children's future are bright; will they be safe? Many of our young boys may not realize it, but their fathers are greatly concerned about them and wish that they could do more for them. As fathers, let us try to set the best example for our children, so that they will be proud to identify with us and what we believe in.

Jacob and Joseph

In concluding this chapter on Jacob and his sons, let me mention something about Jacob and his son Joseph. Allah raised both of them up to prophethood.

Joseph is known for his ability to see beyond the surface; to interpret visions. He was a man of wisdom and insight. Allah blessed him with "Taweel" insight. This ability earned him his freedom from bondage in Egypt and elevated him to a high position as leader over the grain yard in Egypt. Joseph was one of Jacob's twelve sons.

Although Joseph was gifted with the intelligent ability to see behind the veil; he still had to grow in awareness of that ability. Once he was placed in certain circumstances, his awareness of his insight came to fruition.

Where did Joseph get this talent from? He got it from God, but through his father, Jacob, who was also blessed with "Taweel" insight. We inherit some of our father's traits, characteristics, talents and abilities through our genes. Joseph inherited his great insight from his father.

Proof that Jacob had it first is that when Joseph had a dream that eleven stars, the sun and the moon were bowing to him, he went to his father, Jacob for the interpretation and understanding. Joseph did not interpret the dream. He did not know what it meant. The Quran states: *"Behold, Joseph said to his father: Oh my father! I did see eleven stars and the sun and the moon. I saw them prostrate themselves to me. (Jacob) said: 'Oh my son do not tell your vision to your brothers, they may put together a plan against you: For Satan is to man a clear enemy! Thus will your Lord choose you and teach you the interpretation of stories and perfect his favor on you and to the posterity of Jacob. . .* " (12:4-6)

Sometime later, after Joseph had been thrown into a well by his brothers; sold into Egypt; carted into prison; then appointed as the leader over the grain yard; He realized what the dream meant. The reality of what his father taught him manifested before his eyes. *"And he raised his parents upon the throne and they fell down in prostration before him, and he said: Oh my father! This is the fulfillment of my vision of old! My Lord has made it come true!" (12:100)*

One thing that we can learn from this story is that sons should consult with their fathers about things that may be on their mind. Especially if they do not understand it. Another lesson that we can learn is that sometime we may go through several experiences before the opportunity presents itself. And that it takes time for our children to see and understand what we may teach them. We can also learn from this, that our children will inherit some of our better qualities. A profound message that clearly comes out in the story of Joseph is "forgiveness". Joseph forgave his brothers for the wrongs that they had done to him. One of the reasons why they worked against Joseph is because they thought he was more favored by their father, Jacob.

> *"Surely in Joseph and his brothers are a sign for those who seek". (12:7).*

5
Luqman's Advice to His Son

"And certainly We gave wisdom to Luqman . . ."

(31 : 12)

Luqman is a prophet of Allah who was endowed with an abundance of wisdom. He shared his wisdom with his son. The Quran shows us that the first piece of advice that he gave his son, was that he should worship the One God, Allah and that he should not see anything else as important as Allah. *"And when Luqman said to his son while he admonished him: 'Oh my son! Do not associate anything with Allah; most surely making partners with Allah is a great wrong"* (31 : 13)

Luqman went on to inform his son that Allah is aware of all that we do and He is the Knower of things that are hidden. He advised his son to be respectful and kind to his parents. To establish prayer and encourage the doing of good and discourage the doing of evil. To bear patiently with that which may befall him in life. He advised his son not to be arrogant and boastful towards other people. *"And pursue the right course in your going about and lower your voice; surely the most hateful of voices is the braying of the ass" (31;19).*

We should all adhere to Luqman's advice. As fathers, we should share our wisdom with our sons. Although we live in a very complicated and complex world, if we adhere to some basic principles of goodness. And use our intelligence, and trust in Allah above all else, we can make great progress in this world.

6
Knowledge and Education

"Read in the name of your Lord Who created. He created man from a clot. Read and your Lord is the Most Honorable; Who taught (to write) with the pen; Taught man what he did not know" (96:1-5).

"And say, O my Lord! Increase me in knowledge" (20:114).

"Let him who is present impart knowledge to him who is absent"

Prophet Muhammad (SAW)

The more knowledge and education that we obtain the greater is our chance for progress and success. Each generation will go farther down the road of progress if we instill in our children the importance of knowledge and education. One very important way to do that is by making sure that they see you reading and studying sometimes. Start that when they are very young. Let them know that you are always trying to learn. Encourage them to go to the library, by taking them with you. Talk to your children, especially when they are young and very curious about knowledge and education. Try to make them wonder "what is this thing called knowledge that my parents keep talking about?' If we emphasize the importance of knowledge and its value then our children will grow to appreciate knowledge. Most times when children are young they look forward to learning new things and going to that mysterious place called "school".

Education feeds, nourishes and brings out the great potentials that God has created in all of us. It makes possible for us to reach our goals and aspirations. It elevates our minds, and makes us more productive. It increases our worth in society. Education advances the individual, the family and the society.

Every person is obligated to become educated. In Al-Islam, that is made very clear. Muslims are obligated to learn and to share what they learn. It is reported that Prophet Muhammad said "The seeking of knowledge is obligatory upon every Muslim." He also said "knowledge is maintained only through teaching."

What I've been referring to so far was not necessarily

formal education, but the value of knowledge and education itself. Having an appreciation for knowledge and the importance of encouraging our children to love knowledge and education. I make this point because many of our parents and their parents did not have a chance to get much "formal education", but they are very knowledgeable and extremely intelligent and have accomplished a lot, especially in light of their circumstances. They hoped and prayed that their children would have greater opportunities to acquire knowledge and education, than they did.

As parents, we should make sure that we do all that we can to show all of our children that we love them even if one has a Ph.D degree and the other one has no degree. Even if we are proud, and we should be, of the son's educational accomplishments, we must still make sure that both understand that we love them the same. Sometimes it can be difficult to make sure that our children really understand. The best we can do is try.

Formal Education

Educational institutions are an essential part of society. If a people or society expect to advance and compete with other civilizations, then it must have a system of education. Methods and procedures for imparting knowledge is vital because it gives focus and discipline to the student.

Our sons need our help at all levels of education, especially at the secondary level (High School). It is at that level where they really feel a change in themselves and the pressure from others is extremely great. The interest in females becomes a reality. This is a very difficult time for most of our sons. They need our advice, guidance, and education, perhaps, more than any other time. This is when we can really lose them. However, if we can help them get focused, this could be the best time for them and us.

I am a teacher in the Newark School system. I taught Elementary school for three years. I've been teaching High School for seven years. I teach special needs students; mainly those that have been classified as Emotionally Disturbed. Whenever their fathers come to school, I would notice a difference. Even when I was younger, if I knew my father was going to come to school on a certain day, I would act better. I think most of us can relate to that. We should stop by their classes even when they are in elementary school. In fact, we should start then because when they are in the lower grades they are really happy to see you come to their class, even if it is because they misbehaved. They feel proud; they tell their classmates, "that's my dad". Then the next time you go to their class, your child's classmates will say, "That's Hassan's father", or whatever your son's name is.

When I was in high school, I did not do too well academically. The main reason is that I didn't have the proper educational focus. I joined the Nation of Islam in Newark in the early 70s, and as a result of that I had some serious family problems. In addition to that I focused more on working for Muslim businesses, selling <u>Muhammad Speaks</u> newspaper, and the belief that the White man's world, his educational system, etc. was going to soon be destroyed. Another reason is because I really believed that the Blackman only needed five hours of sleep. So I would work at the Steak-N-Take restaurants into late hours of the night and then try to get up in the morning and go to school. Although I would make it to school, I could not concentrate on my classwork because I was too tired. I had no real interest in the "Whiteman's" education. My high school transcript will verify that. If it was not for the fact that God chose Imam W. Deen Mohammed (then called Supreme Minister Wallace D. Muhammad) to be the new leader of the Nation of Islam in 1975 and to bless him with sincerity, wisdom and a sober mind, I would not have finished high school. I was on the verge of dropping out. He gave me a greater sense of reality and the proper focus that I needed to finish high school and college.

To those of us who are fathers, if for some reason you cannot spend a lot of time with your sons, at least, tell them when they have children to spend as much time as they can. Let your sons know that you want to spend more time with them. Don't leave them guessing.

Computers

We live in a computerized society. Therefore, it is a must that our children learn how to operate a computer. We must do all that we can to make sure that our children are exposed to computers. Even if you cannot afford to buy them, take them to the library or the computer room at school. Even if you don't know anything about a computer, make sure your children do. This will help them and us in the future.

College

Colleges and universities are essential for progress in our society. These institutions of higher learning offer us great benefits. The social nature of the college environment can really aid the growth and development of our children. In the college environment, the students are exposed to people from various races, nationalities, religious, economic and social backgrounds. Although their backgrounds may be different their ultimate purpose is the same, that is to acquire knowledge. Life long friendships are also developed. The potential for our children to be exposed to various fields of knowledge is elevated.

The discipline that is required in order to complete college and obtain a degree helps the student better organize his thoughts and ideas.

The college environment also presents a great moral challenge to the student. For most of our children, it is the first time away from home for a long period of time, if he lives on campus; the new freedom can be quite tempting. But if we can help them keep the proper focus then they can handle the challenge. The freedom and the responsibility will make them a better person, especially if they believe in God and see knowledge and education as a gift from God and that it is a means to an end. It is a major step on the road to real freedom and dignity. The more educated our people become, the more progress we will make.

Imam W. Deen Mohammed, speaking at a lecture in

LaGrange, Georgia on March 23, 1997, explained: ". . . We want more freedom to think beyond boundaries that have been established for us. More freedom to exercise our abilities in areas that are, perhaps not even open for us now. So we began to want more freedom . . . We find that education is what makes possible bigger and bigger boundaries for our freedom. Education is the number one liberator for man; and true education, quality education is the gift of God, the Creator."

A Little Advice to the College Student

One of the best ways to achieve in College is to have the right attitude. Be determined to achieve. Join study groups. Try to socialize with people of like mind and attitude. Form your own study group if necessary. The first couple of years may be the most difficult, because of the new environment, the schedule, the procedure, etc. Once you get used to the environment and your professors, and meet some friends it will become easier. But always, remember what you are there for. Believe me, if I made it through college so can you. The reason I say that is because I did not prepare for College, circumstances caused me to go to college and to complete undergraduate in four years. I met people who helped me and so will you. Take advantage of all the programs that are available to all students.

If it doesn't take away from your study, then join some of the student associations and organizations. Above all, don't forget God and keep your focus. If you are a Muslim continue to practice religion. Be wise and use good judgement. It was Al-Islam that helped me make it through college. The discipline that I received from being a member of the Nation of Islam, under the leadership of the Honorable Elijah Muhammad and the new teachings that his son Imam W. Deen Mohammed was giving us all helped me to make it through college.

It is good for the father to come and spend some time with his son while he is in college. This will give you some idea of what campus life is like especially if the father is not a college graduate. It also gives you a chance to be with your son in a different environment. Furthermore it gives your son additional support and it sets a good example for him so that when he has children he may be inclined to do the same thing.

7
Open Communication

"The Most Gracious. Taught the Quran. He created man. He taught him intelligent speech."
(55:1-4)

God has blessed us with the ability to speak; to communicate clearly. We can express ourselves in various ways. We can write, speak or use some kind of sign language to express ourselves.

Talking with our children helps improve our relationship. We should try to avoid just talking to our children when we are angry. We should talk with them, have conversation. Try to be as honest and open as possible. I don't mean just talk about anything. No! Some information can damage them if they are not mentally and emotionally prepared to handle it. We should express our feelings, thoughts and ideas with them. This will encourage them to express their feelings, thoughts and ideas to us more freely. It is better to know what our children are feeling and thinking than not to know.

In many of our families, the sons are afraid of their fathers. Because the father is the strict disciplinarian. So many time he is viewed as the "Bad Guy". This is not to say that we should not be seen as a strong authority figure to our children. Yes, we should be seen that way! That is part of the problem with many of our young boys now, they don't have a strong male figure in their life. But we should also be seen as a compassionate and just father.

We should talk with our children about our religion, about our history. We should talk to them about as many things as we can.

At the Dinner Table

One of the best places to have conversation is at the dinner table when you are all together. Because of the society that we live in with all of its demands and distractions, it is very hard to have everyone at the dinner table at the same time. Many of us eat on the go, we just grab some fast food. But if we can at least try to establish one day a week or every two weeks as the time for dinner and conversation, that will help us a lot.

Walk, Talk and Work

I have found that walking with my children is a very good activity that helps stimulate conversation. Walking in the park with our sons is a very good thing because of the natural environment and serenity. It emphasizes the point that "this is our time". It doesn't have to be a park; it could just be a walk around the block. The idea is to try and find the best situation for you and him to converse. Look for every opportunity to work to stimulate his mind and help his development. Let him work with you on a project. Give him responsibilities. Start him with chores as soon as possible. Having an appreciation for work will take them very far. Keep in mind that Allah is in charge at all times and that we can only try our best to help our children. We must be patient and encourage our children to be patient.

Abdul Khabir Shamsid-Deen, in his book <u>Youth Vision: Out of Darkness Into the Light</u> explains "patience will help you appreciate the value of something. It will also help you develop the strength to endure periods of adversity. When reaching your goal is distant and challenging to reach, patience is your greatest ally . . . growth can't be rushed, it must be accompanied with patience" (Page 11).

Fear Versus Respect

Many of us use fear to keep our children in line. Naturally, parents must assert their authority for the sake of the child's protection and for maintaining order. We don't want our children to be afraid of us. We don't want them to always see us as having the might to hurt them physically.

Love and respect will make our children fear hurting us or

disappointing us. Teaching them to respect their parents and authority by communicating with them and by being an example ourselves is a much better way of helping them than making them fear us. Every new born baby has love and a sacred attachment to its parents. It is the parents' responsibility to nourish and guide that love. Some of our children are actually afraid to even talk to their parents because of the way the parent may react.

Do I Really Know My Son?

Do we really know our children? As fathers, we should ask ourselves the question, "Do I really know my son?" Do you know his likes and dislikes? His pains and joys? Do you have any idea as to what is on his mind? Is he really struggling through life although he looks at peace? Who is he? What does his soul really yearn for? Is he having problems finding a relationship with a female? What are his talents and abilities? Do you know what he really wants to be when he becomes a man? Maybe he's already a man, but you don't know it. Your son may be making the exact same mistake that you made and you don't even know it. He may be on his way to becoming one of the greatest leaders in history and you don't know it.

Think about it!

Do I Really Know My Father?

As sons, we should ask ourselves "Do I really know my

father?" The answer is more likely to be "No!" for the son than it is for the father. It is not because one is more or less interested in knowing about the other one; but mainly because of the fact that the son had no way of seeing his father grow up. Whereas on the other hand, the father has the opportunity to see his son grow up.

What do we really know about our fathers? Do we know what life has really been like for them? Do you really know what his struggles have been before you were born and during your life? Do you know if your father was able to go to school and get an education? Do you know if it was easy or very difficult? What do you know about him? Do you know his greatest desire? Do you know if your father was humiliated by some racist from the south or north, but kept his cool for the sake of the family? Do you know how your father was as a little boy? How were his parents? Have you stopped to think why your father thinks the way he does and acts the way he does? If his behavior is very ugly and displeasing to you; have you thought about why he's like that? And the same if his behavior is beautiful and pleasing to you.

Who is my father? Is he only that man who comes home drunk several days a week? Is he only that man who works hard to provide for his family? What are his fears and hopes? Why won't he express himself? Do you know if the reason why he never told you that he loves you is because his father never told him that. Or because he was raised during a time when that was

seen as something weak and unnecessary. Do you know what he really wants for you in life. Do you know some of his greatest achievements in life? Perhaps it was something that you might consider very simple, but to him it was the greatest thing that ever happened to him.

The more a son learns about his father, the more he learns about himself.

Think about it!

Human Excellence

Whether we know our sons or our fathers or not, we must realize that Allah, God created all of us with a good and honorable nature. Some may have never seen their father but that still does not take away from the decree of God. As a creation of Allah, the potential for growth, development and advancement is inherent in our nature. For some human beings, adversity brings out the best in them. For some people, adversity gives them the will and determination that is needed to thrust them forward.

The Quran says that Almighty God Allah created the human being in the best mold and that He created us in toil and struggle. The Quran also informs us that with difficulty comes ease.

"We have indeed created man in the best of molds" (95:4).

"Surely we have created man in struggle" (90:4).

"Verily with every difficulty there is relief" (94:6).

The Creator has blessed us with intelligence and has raised us above all other creation. He has given us His vast creation as a field for growth. He tells us to think! Reflect! We must use our minds. Encourage our children to use their brains. Think, study, reflect, analyze. Work hard to educate yourself and to develop your soul. Devote time to your inner being. The Quran says of the soul: *He will indeed be suceessful who purifies and spend on it, and he will indeed fail who corrupts or neglects it (91:9-10).*

8
The Link to the Future

"And we left for him among generations (to come) in later times: Peace and Salutation to Abraham". (37:109)

The link to the future for any family or nation is its children. They are the ones who carry us into the future. Our life, hopes, aspirations and plans will be carried on after we are dead and gone, through our offspring. Just as we who are alive now are the link to our ancestors and foreparents, so are our children, our connection to the future. If we want a bright future, then we should invest heavily into our children.

What Will You Leave Your Son?

The plan for the future starts today. As fathers, we must leave a healthy legacy for our children. Fathers must make a strong commitment to leave money, property, positive ideas and a code of behavior for their sons. Leave them a strong foundation upon which they can build their future. Don't only leave them a hope and a dream. Leave them something material to build upon. Tell them "don't die poor!"

Conclusion

In conclusion, let me draw your attention to an excellent example of a father who prepared his son for the future and had faith and trust in his son enough to leave his most cherished work in the hands of one of his sons, even though that son differed with some of his father's ideas and beliefs.

For the sake of those who don't know, I will make it very simple and plain. There was a man named Elijah Muhammad who was appointed as the leader of an organization called the Lost Found Nation of Islam, by his teacher, a man called W.D. Fard. This occurred in the early 30s. Fard was from the "East" Elijah was born in Sandersville, Georgia.

When Elijah's teacher left around 1934, he became the new leader of the Nation of Islam. Elijah worked tirelessly to build his Nation. He received all kinds of attacks and criticisms for what he was trying to do and for what he was teaching. He was sincere and extremely committed to what he believed. He worked very hard, night and day to accomplish his goals. One of his major objectives was to see the African Americans free, independent and dignified.

Over a period of time, thousands of people joined Elijah's organization. Many of them were very sincere, good, well-meaning people. And some were not. The Nation of Islam meant everything to Elijah, it was his life. For about fifty years, he committed himself to that organization. He remained the leader of the Nation of Islam until he died in 1975, after about forty one years of leadership.

What is so heart warming even, twenty two years after his death, is that he left one of his sons, Wallace D. Mohammed as the leader of his organization, the Nation of Islam. That was a real father.   That is an outstanding model of father son relationship in the African American community.

He did not pick Wallace D. Mohammed just because he was his son, but because he knew that Wallace (known today as Imam W. Deen Mohammed) was sincere and could take his community of people, called the Nation of Islam, into the future. He prepared his son, in his own way. Elijah also knew that his son was much like him. He is an independent thinker and a courageous man.

Elijah's son differed with him on the theology of the Nation of Islam. His father excommunicated him several times. In spite of that, and whatever other differences that they may have had as father and son, Elijah chose his son to be the leader of his organization; his pride and joy. Wallace D. Mohammed accepted the responsibility.

It is a blessing to know that you have a son who agrees to carry on the essence of your work. The essence of Elijah's work was for his followers to be true Muslims. Free and independent thinkers and community builders.

Elijah's legacy is preserved in the great works and achievements of his children, particularly his son Imam W. Deen Mohammed who has successfully transformed Elijah's Nation of Islam into a true Muslim community. Whatever accomplishments Imam W. Deen Mohammed and his followers make adds more dignity to Elijah and it carries him into the future. Imam W. Deen Mohammed has shown nothing but love, respect and admiration for his father and his abilities as well as his sincerity and those who followed his father.

It does not always have to be a blood relative who carries your legacy into the future. Many times that person who understands and relates to your goals and aspirations the best are not your blood relatives. It may be that person who is "like a son to me".

I hope that I have written something in this small book that will help father and son relationships and give us a greater reason to "Look to the future".

Bibliography

Ali, A. Yusuf. English Translation, <u>Holy Quran</u>.

El-Amin, Mustafa. <u>Abraham's Legacy: Ancient Wisdom and Modern Reality</u>. New Mind Productions, Jersey City, N.J. 1988.

El-Amin, Mustafa. <u>The Region of Islam and the Nation of Islam: What is the Difference</u>. El-Amin Productions, Newark, N.J. 1990.

Ginzburg, Ralph. <u>100 Years of Lynching</u>. Black Classic Press: Baltimore, MD. 1962.

Kunjufi, Jawanza. <u>Counting the Conspiracy to Destroy Black Boys</u>, Volume 1, African Images, Chicago, Illinois, 1995.

Mohammed, W. Deen <u>Islam's Climate For Business Success</u>, The Sense Maker, Chicago, Illinois, 1995.

Shamsid-Deen, Abdul Khabir. <u>Youth Vision: Out of Darkness Into the Light</u>, Shamsid-Deen Unlimited, Elizabeth, N.J. 1997.

- NOTES -

- NOTES -

- NOTES -

- NOTES -

- NOTES -

- NOTES -

- NOTES -

- NOTES -

- NOTES -

- NOTES -

- NOTES -

- NOTES